AMERICAN

MW01030223

A two-way glossary of words in daily use
on both sides of the Atlantic

ABSON
BOOKS
LONDON 5 Sidney Square London E1 2EY England

For Norman and John

ABSON BOOKS LONDON
5 Sidney Square London E1 2EY England

First published in Great Britain, November 1971
Thirteenth impression September 2001

Compiled and edited by Anthea Bickerton
© Anthea Bickerton and Pat McCormack
Cover design by Chris Bird
Photography by Patrick Harrison

Printed by Gutenberg Press, Malta
ISBN 0 902920 60X

PREFACE

The words in this glossary have been selected because of the confusion or misinterpretation they can cause on one or other side of the Atlantic. Primarily this book is for the visitor to Britain or America, but it is also for the Englishman who heard about *denatured alcohol* and thought it was alcohol with water added, and for the wife of an American airman stationed in Suffolk who combed the local shops for a *jelly roll*.

There are many surprises and even pitfalls in our once common language and I hope this glossary will help people to be more linguistically mobile, but not so mobile that when they cross the Atlantic all possibility of amusing situations is entirely ironed out.

My apologies to those who think there are words missing from this glossary. Suggestions for future editions from anyone who feels impassioned enough to write will be very much appreciated.

Meanwhile my thanks go to the team of contributors who have lived on both sides of the *pond*.

Anthea Bickerton

CONTENTS

AMERICAN—ENGLISH

AMERICAN	ENGLISH
account	bill/account
adhesive tape	sticking plaster
aisle	gangway
antenna	aerial *(radio/TV)*
apartment/unit	flat
apartment hotel	service flats
apartment house	block of flats

AMERICAN	ENGLISH
baby bed/crib	cot/crib
baby carriage/baby buggy	pram *(perambulator)*
back-up lights	reversing lights
baggage room	left luggage office
balcony *(theater)*	gallery
barette	hairslide
baseboard	skirting board
bathe *(v.)*	bath
bathrobe	dressing gown

AMERICAN	ENGLISH
bathtub	bath
bell pepper	green pepper
bill	bank note
billfold	wallet
billion = **thousand million**	billion = million million
bobbie pin	hair grip/kirby grip
bomb *(disaster)*	bomb *(success)*
booth *(telephone)*	kiosk *(telephone/cigarette)*
broil	grill
buffet	sideboard
bureau	chest of drawers
business suit	lounge suite

call/phone	ring up/phone
call collect	reverse charges
can	tin
candy	sweets/chocolate
candy store	sweet shop/confectioner

AMERICAN	ENGLISH
caravan	convoy
carnival	fair *(fun)*
change purse	purse
charged *(goods bought)*	put down/entered
check *(restaurant)*	bill
checkers	draughts
check room	cloakroom
cheese cloth	butter muslin/cheese cloth
chicory	endive
chips *(potato)*	crisps
city/municipal government	corporation
closet	cupboard
closet *(hanging clothes)*	wardrobe
clothes pin	clothes peg
collar button	collar stud
collar stay	collar stiffener
comforter	eiderdown
concert master	leader

AMERICAN	ENGLISH
conductor	guard *(railway)*
connect *(telephone)*	put through
cookie	biscuit *(sweet)*
corn starch	corn flour
cotton batting/ absorbent cotton	cotton wool
cotton candy	candy floss
cracker	biscuit *(unsweetened)*
crazy bone	funny bone
cream of wheat	semolina
cuffs *(pants)*	turn-ups *(trousers)*
custom made	bespoke/made to measure

davenport/couch	sofa
dead-end	cul-de-sac
deck *(cards)*	pack
delivery truck	van
denatured alcohol	methylated spirits

AMERICAN	ENGLISH
derby	bowler/hard hat
desk clerk	receptionist
dessert	pudding/dessert
detour	diversion
diaper	nappy
dime store/five and ten	Woolworths
dishes, do the	wash up
divided highway	dual carriageway
down town	centre *(city/business)*
draft	conscription
drapes	curtains
dresser	chest of drawers
druggist	chemist
drugstore/pharmacy	chemist's shop
drygoods store	draper
dump *(n. and v.)*	tip
dungarees	jeans
duplex	semi-detached

AMERICAN	ENGLISH
editorial	leader
eggplant	aubergine
electric cord/wire	flex
elevator	lift
endive	chicory
eraser	rubber/india rubber
eyeball *(v.)*	visually position

faculty	staff
fall	autumn
faucet	tap
fender	wing/mudguard
first balcony	upper circle
first floor	ground floor
flashlight	torch/flashlight
floor lamp	standard lamp
floor walker	shop walker
freeway/super highway	motorway

AMERICAN	ENGLISH
freight truck	goods truck
French fries	chips
freshman *(at university)*	1st year undergraduate
front desk *(hotel)*	reception

AMERICAN	ENGLISH
garbage/trash	rubbish
garbage can/ash can/ trash can	dustbin/bin
garter belt	suspender belt
garters	suspenders
gas	petrol
gas station	filling station
gear shift	gear lever
generator	dynamo
German shepherd/ police dog	alsation
goose bumps	goose pimples
grade	class/form

AMERICAN	ENGLISH
grade crossing	level crossing
green thumb	green fingers
ground wire	earth wire/earth
hamburger bun	bap
hamburger meat	mince
hardware store	ironmonger
hat check girl	cloakroom attendant
homely – ugly	homely – pleasant
hood *(car)*	bonnet
hope chest	bottom drawer
hotdog bun	bridge roll
housewares	hardware
hutch	Welsh dresser
incorporated	limited
information/directory assistance	directory enquiries
intermission	interval

AMERICAN	ENGLISH
J	
jail	gaol/jail
janitor	caretaker/porter
jelly roll	Swiss roll
jump rope	skipping rope
junior	3rd year *(school)*
K	
kerosene	paraffin
knickers	plus-fours
knock up	make pregnant/put in the family way
lawyer/attorney	solicitor
leader	leading article in newspaper/ 1st violin in orchestra
lease/rent	let
legal holiday	bank holiday
licence plate	number plate
lima bean	broad bean

AMERICAN	ENGLISH
line *(n.)*	queue
line-up	identification parade
liquor	spirits
liquor store	off licence/wine merchant
liverwurst	liver sausage
living room	sitting room/lounge/ drawing room/living room
lobby/foyer	foyer
long distance	trunk call
lost and found	lost property
love seat	settee
lumber room	box room

AMERICAN	ENGLISH
mail *(n.)*	post
mail box/mail drop	pillar box
mailman	postman
make reservation	book
meat grinder	mincer

AMERICAN	ENGLISH
median strip/divider	centre reservation
mezzanine/loge	dress circle
molasses	black treacle
monkey wrench	spanner
motorbike	moped
motorcycle	motorbike/motorcycle
movie	film
movie house/theatre	cinema
moving van	pantechnicon/removal van
Mr. J. Jones	J. Jones Esq./Mr. J. Jones
muffler	silencer
mutual fund	unit trust

newsdealer/news stand	newsagent
nightstick	truncheon
nipple	teat
notions	haberdashery

AMERICAN	ENGLISH
odometer	mileometer
office *(doctor's/dentist's)*	surgery
oil pan	sump
one way ticket	single ticket
orchestra seats	stalls
outlet/socket	point/power point
overalls	dungarees
overpass	flyover
pacifier	dummy
package	parcel
paddle *(ping pong)*	bat
pantie hose	tights
pantry	larder
pants/slacks	trousers/slacks
parka	anorak
parking lot	car park
pass *(vehicle, etc.)*	overtake/pass

AMERICAN	ENGLISH
pavement	road
penitentiary	prison
period	full-stop
person-to-person	personal call
phonograph/record player	gramophone/record player
pit *(fruit)*	stone
pitcher	jug
pollywog	tadpole
popsicle	iced lolly
pot holders/gloves	oven gloves/cloth
powdered sugar/ confectioner's sugar	icing sugar
precinct	district
president *(business)*	chairman
principal	headmaster/mistress
private school	public school/private school
public school	state school
pull-off	lay-by
pullman/sleeper	sleeping car

AMERICAN	ENGLISH
pump	court shoe
purse/pocket book	handbag

AMERICAN	ENGLISH
raincheck	postponement
raincoat	mackintosh
raisin	sultana
realtor	estate agent
rear view mirror	wing mirror
recess	break *(school)*
restroom	toilet/cloakroom *(indoors)*
rest room/toilet/ comfort station	public convenience *(outdoors)*
rhinestone	diamanté
roast	joint *(meat)*
robin *(large red-breasted bird, symbol – first sign of Spring)*	robin *(small red-breasted bird, symbol of Christmas)*
roller coaster	big dipper
roomer	lodger

AMERICAN	ENGLISH
round trip ticket	return ticket
rubber	contraceptive
rubber cement	cow gum
rubbing alcohol	surgical spirit
run *(for public office)*	stand
rutabaga/turnip	swede

sack lunch	packed lunch
sales clerk/sales girl	shop assistant
scab	blackleg
scallion	spring onion *(similar)*
schedule	time-table
scotch tape	sellotape
scratch pad	scribbling pad/block
second floor	first floor
sedan	saloon car
semester *(school – two in a year)*	term *(three in a year)*
senior	4th year *(school)*

AMERICAN	ENGLISH
sewer pipe/soil pipe	drain *(indoor)*
shade *(window)*	blind
sheers/under drapes	net curtains
sherbet	ice/sorbet
shoestring	bootlace/shoelace
shorts/jockey shorts	briefs
shorts *(underwear)*	pants
shot *(injection)*	jab
shredded *(coconut)*	desiccated
sideburns	sideboards
sidewalk	pavement/footpath
sled	sledge/toboggan
slice *(bacon)*	rasher
slingshot	catapult
smoked herring	kipper
snaps	press studs
sneakers/tennis shoes	gym shoes/plimsolls/ tennis shoes
soccer	football/soccer

AMERICAN	ENGLISH
soda cracker	cream cracker
spatula/pancake turner	fish slice
spool	cotton reel
squash	marrow *(similar)*
stand in line/line up	queue
station wagon	estate car
stop lights/traffic signals/ stop signals	traffic lights
stove	cooker
straight *(drink)*	neat
stroller	pushchair
sub-division	housing estate
subway	tube/underground
suspenders	braces
sweater/pullover	jumper/sweater/pullover

tag	label
tea cart	tea trolley

AMERICAN	ENGLISH
Texas gate	cattle grid
thread	cotton
thumb tack	drawing pin
tic-tac-toe	noughts and crosses
time payment/instalment plan	hire purchase
toilet/john/bathroom	lavatory/toilet/w.c.
top *(car)*	roof/hood
traffic circle	round-about/island
trailer/camper/mobile home	caravan
trailer truck	articulated lorry
tramp/call girl/hooker/street walker	prostitute/tart/whore
truck	lorry
trunk/rear deck *(car)*	boot
tube	valve
two weeks	fortnight

Toque - wool hat

AMERICAN	ENGLISH

undergraduates:
  freshman — 1st year undergraduate
  sophomore — 2nd year undergraduate
  junior — 3rd year undergraduate
  senior — 4th year undergraduate
undershirt — vest
underwear *(washing)* — smalls

vacation — holiday
vacuum *(v.)* — hoover
vacuum cleaner — hoover
valence — pelmet
vest — waistcoat

wall to wall — fitted carpet/wall to wall
wash cloth — face flannel
wash up — wash your hands

AMERICAN	ENGLISH
water heater *(electric)*	immersion heater
water heater *(gas)*	geyser
weather stripping	draught excluder
wharf/pier	quay *(pron. 'key')*
windbreaker	windcheater
windshield	windscreen
wire	telegram
with or without? *(milk/cream in coffee)*	black or white?

yard	garden

zee	zed
zero	nought
zip code	postal code
zucchini	courgettes

ENGLISH—AMERICAN

	ENGLISH	AMERICAN
A	**aerial** *(radio/TV)*	antenna
	alsation	German shepherd/police dog
	anorak	parka
	articulated lorry	trailer truck
	aubergine	eggplant
	autumn	fall
B	**bank holiday**	legal holiday
	bank note	bill
	bap	hamburger bun
	bat *(ping pong)*	paddle
	bath	bathtub
	bath *(v.)*	bathe
	bespoke/made to measure	custom made
	big dipper	roller coaster
	bill	check *(restaurant)*
	bill/account	account
	billion = **million million**	billion = thousand million
	biscuit *(sweet)*	cookie

bicks - biscuits

28

ENGLISH	AMERICAN
biscuit *(unsweetened)*	cracker
black or white?	
(milk/cream in coffee)	with or without?
blackleg	scab
black treacle	molasses
blind *(window)*	shade
block of flats	apartment house/building
blue jeans	dungarees
bomb *(success)*	bomb *(disaster)*
bonnet *(car)*	hood
book *(v.)*	make reservation
boot *(car)*	trunk/rear deck
bootlace/shoelace	shoestring
bottom drawer	hope chest
bowler/hard hat	derby
box room	lumber room
braces	suspenders
break *(school)*	recess
bridge roll	hotdog bun

ENGLISH	AMERICAN
briefs	shorts *(jockey shorts)*
broad bean	lima bean
butter muslin/cheese cloth	cheese cloth

ENGLISH	AMERICAN
candy floss	cotton candy
caravan	trailer
caretaker/porter	janitor
car park	parking lot
catapult	slingshot
cattle grid	Texas gate
centre *(city/business)*	downtown
centre reservation	median strip/divider
chairman *(business)*	president
chemist	druggist
chemist's shop	pharmacy/drugstore
chest of drawers	dresser/bureau
chicory	endive
chips	French fries

ENGLISH	AMERICAN
chocolate/sweets	candy
cinema	movie house/theater
class/form *(school)*	grade
cloakroom	check room
cloakroom attendant	hat check girl
clothes peg	clothes pin
collar stiffener	collar stay
collar stud	collar button
conscription	draft
contraceptive	rubber
convoy	caravan
cooker	stove
corn flour	corn starch
corporation	city/municipal government
cot/crib	baby bed/crib
cotton	thread
cotton reel	spool
cotton wool	cotton batting/absorbent cotton

ENGLISH	AMERICAN
courgettes	zucchini
court shoe	pump
cow gum	rubber cement
cream cracker	soda cracker
crisps	chips *(potato)*
cul-de-sac	dead end
cupboard	closet
curtains	drapes

desiccated *(coconut)*	shredded
diamanté	rhinestone
directory enquiries	information/directory assistance
district	precinct
diversion	detour
drain *(indoors)*	sewer pipe/soil pipe
draper	drygoods store
draught excluder	weather stripping

ENGLISH	AMERICAN
draughts	checkers
drawing pin	thumb tack
dress circle	mezzanine/loge
dressing-gown	bathrobe
dual carriageway	divided highway
dummy	pacifier
dungarees	overalls
dustbin/bin	garbage can/ash can/
	trash can
dynamo	generator

earth wire/earth	ground wire
eiderdown	comforter
endive	chicory
Esq./Mr.	Mr.
estate agent	realtor
estate car	station wagon

ENGLISH	AMERICAN

F

face flannel	wash cloth
fair *(fun)*	carnival
filling station	gas station
film	movie
first floor	second floor
fish slice	pancake spatula/turner
fitted carpet	wall to wall
flat	apartment
flex	electric cord/wire
fly-over	overpass
football/soccer	soccer
fortnight	two weeks
foyer	lobby/foyer
full stop *(punc.)*	period
funny bone	crazy bone

G

gallery *(theatre)*	balcony
gangway	aisle

frock dress

ENGLISH	AMERICAN
gaol	jail
garden	yard
gear lever	gear shift
geyser *(gas)*	water heater
goods truck *(railway)*	freight truck
goose pimples	goose bumps
gramophone/record player	phonograph/record player
green fingers	green thumb
green pepper/capsicum	bell pepper/green pepper/sweet pepper
grill *(v.)*	broil
guard *(railway)*	conductor
gym shoes/plimsolls/tennis shoes	sneakers/tennis shoes

haberdashery	notions
hair grip/kirby grip	bobbie pin
hair slide	barette

ENGLISH	AMERICAN
handbag	purse/pocket book
hardware	housewares
headmaster/mistress	principal
hire purchase	time payment/instalment plan
holiday	vacation
homely – pleasant	homely – ugly
hoover *(n.)*	vacuum cleaner
hoover *(v.)*	vacuum
housing estate	sub-division
ice/sorbet	sherbet
iced lolly	popsicle
icing sugar	powdered sugar/confectioner's sugar
identification parade	line-up
immersion heater *(electric)*	water heater
interval	intermission
ironmonger	hardware store

ENGLISH	AMERICAN
jab *(injection)*	shot
joint *(meat)*	roast
jug	pitcher
jumper/sweater/pullover	sweater/pullover
kiosk *(telephone/cigarette)*	booth *(telephone)*
kipper	smoked herring
knock up	to call *(from sleep)*
knock up *(tennis)*	warm up
label	tag
larder	pantry
lavatory/toilet/w.c.	toilet/john/bathroom
lay-by	pull-off
leader:	
(1) leading article in newspaper	editorial
(2) 1st violin in orchestra	concert master
left luggage office	baggage room

ENGLISH	AMERICAN
let	lease/rent
level crossing *(railway)*	grade crossing
lift	elevator
limited *(company)*	incorporated
liver sausage	liverwurst
lodger	roomer
lorry	truck
lost property	lost and found
lounge suit	business suit

lounge – sitting room

ENGLISH	AMERICAN
mackintosh	raincoat
marrow	squash *(similar)*
methylated spirits	denatured alcohol
mileometer	odometer
mince	hamburger meat
mincer	meat grinder
moped	motorbike
motorway	freeway/throughway/ super highway

	ENGLISH	AMERICAN

neeps - turnips

N

nappy	diaper
neat *(drink)*	straight
net curtains	sheers/under drapes
newsagent	news dealer/news stand
nought	zero
noughts and crosses	tic-tac-toe
number plate	licence plate

O

off licence/wine merchant	liquor store
off-side lane	right-hand lane nearest centre
	- of road—in Britain
oven cloth/gloves	pot holders/gloves
overtake *(vehicle)*	pass

P

pack *(of cards)*	deck
packed lunch	sack lunch
pantechnicon	moving van

39

ENGLISH	AMERICAN
pants	shorts *(underwear)*
paraffin	kerosene
parcel	package
pavement/footpath	sidewalk
pelmet	valence
personal call	person-to-person
petrol	gas *(-oline)*
pillar box	mail box/mail drop
plus-fours	knickers
point/power point	outlet/socket
post	mail
postal code	zip code
postman	mailman
postponement	raincheck
pram	baby carriage/baby buggy
press studs	snaps
prison	penitentiary
prostitute/tart/whore	tramp/call girl/hooker/ street walker

ENGLISH	AMERICAN
public convenience	restroom/toilet/comfort station
public school/private school	private school
pudding	dessert
purse	change purse
pushchair	stroller
put down/entered *(goods bought)*	charged
put through *(telephone)*	connect

quay	wharf/pier
queue *(n.)*	line
queue *(v.)*	stand in line/line up

rasher *(bacon)*	slice
reception *(hotel)*	front desk

ENGLISH	AMERICAN
receptionist	desk clerk
return ticket	round trip ticket
reverse charges	call collect
reversing lights	back up lights
ring up	call/phone
robin *(small red-breasted bird, symbol of Christmas)*	robin *(large red-breasted bird, symbol—first sign of Spring)*
roof/hood *(car)*	top
roundabout *(road)*	traffic circle
rubbish	garbage/trash

ENGLISH	AMERICAN
saloon *(car)*	sedan
scribbling pad/block	scratch pad
sellotape	scotch tape
semi-detached	duplex
semolina	cream of wheat
service flats	apartment hotel

ENGLISH	AMERICAN
settee	love seat
shop assistant	sales clerk/sales girl
shop walker	floor walker
sideboard	buffet
sideboards *(hair)*	sideburns
silencer *(car)*	muffler
single ticket	one way ticket
sitting room/living room/ lounge/drawing room	living room
skipping rope	jump rope
skirting board	baseboard
sledge/toboggan	sled
sleeping car	pullman/sleeper
smalls *(washing)*	underwear
sofa	davenport/couch
solicitor	lawyer/attorney
sorbet	sherbet
spanner	monkey wrench
spirits *(drink)*	liquor

ENGLISH	AMERICAN
spring onion	scallion *(similar)*
staff *(academic)*	faculty
stalls *(theatre)*	orchestra seats
stand *(for public office)*	run
standard lamp	floor lamp
state school	public school
sticking plaster	adhesive tape
stone *(fruit)*	pit
sultana	raisin
sump *(car)*	oil pan
surgery *(doctor's/dentist's)*	office
surgical spirit	rubbing alcohol
suspender belt	garter belt
suspenders	garters
swede	turnip/rutabaga
sweet shop/confectioner	candy store
sweets/chocolate	candy
Swiss roll	jelly roll

ENGLISH	AMERICAN

ENGLISH	AMERICAN
tadpole	pollywog
tap	faucet
teat *(baby's bottle)*	nipple
tea trolley	tea cart
telegram	wire
term *(academic—three in a year)*	semester *(two in a year)*
tights	pantie hose
time-table	schedule
tin	can
tip *(n. and v.)*	dump
torch	flashlight
traffic lights	stop lights/traffic signals/ stop signals
trousers	pants/slacks
truncheon *(police)*	night stick
trunk call	long distance
tube/underground	subway
turn-ups *(trousers)*	cuffs *(pants)*

	ENGLISH	AMERICAN
U	**Undergraduates:**	
	1st year	freshman
	2nd year	sophomore
	3rd year	junior
	4th year	senior
	unit trust	mutual fund
	upper circle	first balcony
V	**valve** *(radio)*	tube
	van	delivery truck
	van *(car type)*	panel truck
	vest	undershirt
	visually position	eyeball *(v.)*
W	**waistcoat**	vest
	wallet	billfold
	wardrobe	closet
	wash up	do the dishes

ENGLISH	AMERICAN
wash your hands	wash up
Welsh dresser	hutch
windcheater	windbreaker
windscreen	windshield
wing/mudguard	fender
Woolworths	dime store/five and ten
zed	zee

By cracky

Bonnie lovely clever

Other titles available from Abson Books London

Language Glossaries:
American English/English American
Australian English/English Australian
Irish English/English Irish
Lancashire English
Rhyming Cockney Slang
Yiddish English/English Yiddish
Yorkshire English
A Queer Companion (A rough guide to Gay slang)
Ultimate Language of Flowers
Scouse English
Geordie English
The Death of Kings (A medical history of the Kings & Queens of England)

Literary Quiz & Puzzle Books:
Jane Austen
Brontë Sisters
Charles Dickens
Gilbert & Sullivan
Thomas Hardy
Sherlock Holmes
Shakespeare

All the above titles are available from good booksellers or by contacting the publisher.

ABSON BOOKS LONDON
5 Sidney Square London E1 2EY
Tel: 0171 790 4737   Fax: 0171 790 7346
e-mail: absonbooks@aol.com